D0603353

Dad — Merry Christmas!
Enjoy reading about &
listening to your friend
"Hamp"! love,
Jenifer
Dec.
2015

Flying Home

Lionel Hampton

CELEBRATING 100 YEARS OF GOOD VIBES

Flying Home
ISBN: 978-0-681-81754-8

State Street Press
An Imprint of Borders Group, Inc.
100 Phoenix Drive
Ann Arbor, MI 48108
www.borders.com

© Copyright State Street Press 2008
All rights reserved.

No part of this book may be used or reproduced by any means, graphic,
electronic, or mechanical, including photocopying, recording, taping or
by any information storage retrieval system without written permission of
the publisher. No transmittal in any form or by any means allowed without
written permission from the publisher, except in the case of quotations
embodied in press, articles and reviews.

This edition is published by State Street Press
by special arrangement with

The Cadence Group, LLC
3906 Oak Street
Cincinnati, OH 45227
www.thecadencegrp.com

Printed and manufactured in Malaysia

Cover Photo: AP Images
Cover Design: Gwyn Kennedy Snider
Interior Design and Layout: GKS Creative
Editor: Amy Collins
Contributor: Leslie Bolton

Flying Home
Lionel Hampton

WRITTEN BY STANLEY CROUCH | FOREWORD BY WYNTON MARSALIS

CELEBRATING 100 YEARS OF GOOD VIBES

State Street Press

© Herman Leonard Photography LLC/ctsimages.com

All Over the Universe, Hamp is Still Playing

INTRODUCTION BY WYNTON MARSALIS

It is more than an honor to be asked to offer my thoughts in this book celebrating the one hundredth birthday of Lionel Hampton. Lionel was a man whose greatness is beyond question, a man who carried the joyous message of jazz from city to city and country to country for over seven glorious decades.

I have been fortunate to meet, to hear, and to play with the best musicians from many eras. The greatest jazzmen have a unique spiritual energy that you can feel in an audience, at a rehearsal, and especially on the bandstand. It is if they are possessed. What they are possessed by can elevate the quality of your life.

Lionel Hampton was one of the most remarkable musicians because he had something that made him more than just unique. He was a pyromaniac of swing. You could depend on him to set fires on bandstands all over the world all night long. He started off hot and got hotter as the night wore on and pretty soon it was time to call the fire department. Hamp was still playing.

Of course, Hamp was famous for his fiery, extended concerts. But that was only one side of Lionel Hampton. I once heard him play in an ancient Roman arena in Nice, France. The sun was going down and the people were screaming for an encore.

Hamp seized this moment of natural beauty to play a solo piece. He played "La Vie En Rose" and every note rang with the bittersweet essence that can only come from the soul of a grand master. As the sun set and the night began to darken, it seemed as if every phrase that Hamp sent rising into the evening had the romantic feeling of so many twilights. He was beautiful like that. And the people loved him.

Lionel Hampton was a man who didn't spend his time talking about the past unless it told you something about the present. He was wholly interested in how the extensive knowledge of jazz veterans could be used to help educate musicians and audiences alike. He believed in a hands-on approach to education, and was committed to teaching young musicians. He knew the glory that comes with being able to play. He was well acquainted with that glory because he communicated it to audiences of every era from the 1920s until his death.

Lionel Hampton was one of the most gifted musicians to ever play jazz. He was a true improviser with a natural gift for melody. He possessed a dedication and special energy that pushed an already first class talent up into the rarefied air of jazz heaven. Everyone knew Hamp could play, but it was hard to comprehend just how much he could play. He stayed current. His talent was broad and took up a surprising amount of musical space. Hamp was the only one from his generation who could — or would — play through Coltrane's harmonic innovations like "Giant Steps" and "Moment's Notice." Then he might turn around and play the hell out of "Stardust" in a definitive swing era style. He played an ever expanding range of material with absolute authority.

No matter how late it was, he would turn to you and say "Let's play one more, Gates."

All over the universe, Hamp is still playing in the twilight with the audience screaming for more.

Wynton Marsalis

Lionel

Before the legend, there was the man.

Lionel Hampton was born on April 20, 1908, in Louisville, Kentucky, though he spent very little time there. Shortly after he was born, his mother moved back to her hometown of Birmingham, Alabama, where Hampton was raised by the matriarch of the family, his beloved and influential grandmother. His "mama," as he called her, condensed life down to two simple tenets: faith in God and the need for a good education. Hampton often told people that her faith was so strong, she was able to heal his childhood bout of appendicitis with castor oil and prayer.

Hampton was very proud of how dedicated his family was to education and recalls what his grandmother said to him after his aunt graduated from high school, "Now you see how beautiful it is to graduate." These twin forces of faith and education would mold the musician into a man with a vision. It was during a church service that Lionel first picked up a mallet and beat a drum. He felt that "drumming was the best way to get close to God."

Hampton openly acknowledged the unfair system of segregation that prevailed in his youth, but recalls most clearly the various ways in which the black community in Alabama not only held onto but expressed its humanity in style. The black Birmingham community shared with Lionel its optimism, humility, discipline, vitality, and spiritual confidence; the same qualities that made Hampton so impressive as a man.

Following World War I, Lionel's grandmother decided to move the family to Chicago, creating yet another progressive movement in young Hampton's education in both music and life. His grandmother knew he would get a better education up north, but she could have never predicted the sensations the city was about to nurture in Lionel. Jazz permeated the air in Chicago during those days and Lionel's Uncle Richard was already deep into the jazz scene. Richard made his way in the world supplying liquor during prohibition and got to know all the best musicians in town when they came to play at his famous parties.

During this time, jazz crossed the threshold from the streets outside. Lionel was able to meet several great jazz artists at his uncle's many parties. Jazz was more than just in his blood; it was infused in his soul.

The public schools in Chicago didn't pass his grandmother's standard of acceptability, so she sent him away to a Catholic school, despite the fact that the family did not practice Catholicism. It was here that Lionel learned the rudiments of drumming while participating in the fife and drum corps. Of course, Lionel being the curious and exuberant boy that he was, could not help but try his hand at other instruments, such as the xylophone, timpani, and orchestra bells.

When Lionel returned to Chicago a little over a year later, he forayed deeper into the music world by joining the Chicago Defender Youth Band under the direction of Major N. Clark Smith. He took a job as a newsboy and sacrificed his Saturday afternoons just so he could play in the band. Here he received ear training and learned harmony. He experimented with several different instruments but honed his talent for the drums.

Young Hampton began to make a reputation for himself at the drums. He had such a good reputation for creating a great beat that his old high school mate, Les Hite, sent for Lionel to join his band in Los Angeles. Still in high school, Hamp needed his grandmother's permission to go west. "Mama"

©2003 International Jazz Collections, Special Collections & Archives, University of Idaho, Moscow, Idaho.

Lionel Hampton's family photograph.
Lionel is the young boy in white shirt and tie.

of the first vibraphone solos, "Memories of You," with Louis Armstrong in October of 1930. At the time that Armstrong was visiting the West Coast, he was the most influential frontiersman in what was then the still relatively new art form of jazz. The trumpeter had enormous physical power and imagination and, according to Armstrong, he would sometimes blow his horn in situations that were hot in so many ways that he could literally hear his socks squishing in his shoes. That kind of unbridled power was something that Hampton picked up on and took to the many successive bandstands where he achieved so much glory, either as a sideman or a leader, an employee or an employer.

During that same period, Hampton met Gladys, the woman who would one day be his wife. A sophisticated and well-known business woman who made her reputation as a couture seamstress to the stars, Gladys immediately saw Lionel's talent and potential and took him under her wing.

apparently thought that getting away from Uncle Richard's "parties" would be good for Lionel and gave her consent. She allowed him to leave school under the condition that he promise to get his high school diploma out in California. A few days later, Lionel was on a train heading to Los Angeles.

After a brief but difficult time in which he had to soldier through short wages, Hampton shot to the top so fast his head must have felt as though it was on a swivel. He began to get work in society bands and in jazz bands which also played for dancers. Hampton was loved because he could lift the bandstand with his strong control of tempos and his hot rhythms. He could excite the dancers who loved the heavy after-beat that pushed them to the ballroom floors. Lionel was quickly becoming the king of rooms where the dancers were, as Dizzy Gillespie once said, "the mirrors of the music."

Not long after he started moving up the ranks in Los Angeles, he started working for and recording with the very hottest star in jazz, Louis Armstrong. Hampton became known on a national and international basis when he recorded one

*Jazz was more
than just in his blood;
it was infused in his soul.*

Like any young man shown some attention by a good-looking and sophisticated woman, Hampton took interest but actually was more impressed with her good business sense and the fact that she had been well educated at Fisk University. She was what was then known as a "career woman." The intelligent young beauty advised Hampton to save his money and tread carefully in show business.

When Armstrong returned to New York in 1931, Gladys began to get chummier with Hampton, who remained in Los Angeles, and became his unofficial manager. She negotiated so well for him that other black musicians asked her to represent them as well. Soon, according to Hampton, they were the best paid musicians in a town where it was customary for black

A promotional photo taken during his early years as a professional musician.

Lionel's grandmother let him leave school and join his friend, Les Hite, in Los Angeles under the condition that Lionel finish school out in California.

LH 0190, International Jazz Collections, Special Collections & Archives, University of Idaho, Moscow, Idaho.

musicians to receive salaries that were no more than twenty percent of what white musicians were paid.

Hampton's career picked up momentum in Los Angeles. His popularity increased and a reputation began to spread among musicians who either knew or had heard of the swinging drummer who could double on the odd instrument that had evolved from the xylophone through the use of electricity. To make good on the promise he had made his grandmother, Hampton went to finish high school through an extension program at the University of Southern California. At the university, Hampton was also able to enroll in music classes where he studied harmony and theory, both of which allowed him to understand the logic of the melodies invented by jazz musicians whom he admired. He had always been able to clearly hear the notes, but he began to learn why they were there in the first place. It was this education that was the basis for the logic that always comes through in his finest improvisations, no matter how heated.

Lionel Hampton was a success, as a man and as a musician. But this was just the beginning. Soon, his career would really start to fly.

It was Louie Armstrong who gave Hampton his nickname. While performing with the New Cotton Club Orchestra in LA, Armstrong worked with Lionel. One night, he turned to Hampton and said "You swing so good, I'm going to call you "Gates."

Later that month, while in a recording session, Armstrong asked Lionel to try his hand at the newly delivered instrument in the corner...the vibraphone.

Lionel with his classmates in an undated photo. Lionel's grandmother was determined to see him get a good education. She sent him to Holy Rosary Academy in Wisconsin to remove Lionel from the distractions of music and the family bootlegging business. Later, he returned to Chicago to attend St. Monica's and became a member of Major Nathaniel Clark Smith's Chicago Defender band.

Bessie Smith was a frequent visitor to the Chicago jazz parties thrown by Lionel's uncle Richard. Richard organized regular jam sessions at his house for musicians and singers. Jelly Roll Morton, Louis Armstrong, Ma Rainey, Bix Beiderbecke, and Frank Teschemacher all played at "Uncle Richard's."

Young Lionel once got so emotional when Bessie was singing that he was kicked out of the room!

Years later, uncle Richard drew attention by being the driver in the car crash that ended Bessie's life.

Buddy Rich making it happen on the drums.

James Moody was a regular at
"Uncle Richard's" parties.

© Herman Leonard Photography LLC/ctsimages.com

The Four Horsemen

Lionel was happy to be playing in Los Angeles and was picking up a number of semi-steady gigs; but Gladys kept after Hampton until she had convinced him that he could be successful with his own band. He eventually agreed to take a chance and threw his hat in the bandleader's ring, traveling up and down the West Coast. He had both talent and dedication, but times were hard for black musicians. Segregation was in full force. The band was not allowed through the front door of most restaurants; if they wanted to order, they had to get takeout from the back. Accommodations ranged from flea-ridden boarding houses to camping out in the car. Undeterred, Hampton pressed on.

Though he had gained some popularity along the coast with radio play, he was not becoming as successful as Gladys had hoped. Never easily discouraged, Gladys told everyone she met that she was sure that the public would develop an appetite for Lionel's gifts when the time was right.

Hanging up the road tour, Hampton got a steady gig at the Paradise Nightclub in Los Angeles. There he had the freedom to experiment and try out new sounds, and he spent most of his time studying the vibes. He sharpened his style and succeeded in transforming the vibraphone into a jazz instrument. Hampton's creativity lured the public in and the joint was packed night after night. As the crowds were gaining an appreciation for his unique musical style, Hampton was beginning to enjoy his ever-increasing fame. Then one night,

John Hammond showed up. Lionel didn't know it yet, but walking through the door with Hammond was Hampton's future as one of the pioneers of integrated jazz.

John Hammond was a wealthy white man from New York who had been drawn to jazz ever since his black nanny took him as a child to see stage shows in Harlem. Outside of the musicians themselves, Hammond had become the most impressive talent scout in the world of jazz and was a record producer known for consistently high quality sessions.

Hammond had always been disturbed by the racial prejudices of the day. Musicians of all hues and creeds often played together in relaxed, private jam sessions, but black and white musicians could not play together in public.

Hammond was close to Benny Goodman, who was visiting Los Angeles to play the Palomar. Goodman was taken to hear Hampton and was so thrilled by what he heard that the great clarinetist got up on the bandstand and jammed with Hampton through the night. The very next night, Goodman brought along pianist Teddy Wilson and drummer Gene Krupa, and they started wailing. Goodman was pleased with the sound and asked Hampton to join them in a recording session.

Hammond suggested to Goodman that he take Hampton back to New York and expand his already integrated trio into a quartet that would have two black men, Teddy Wilson and Hampton, featured with Goodman and Gene Krupa.

Played by Lionel Hampton at the University of Idaho
Jazz Festival in honor of jazz great, Benny Goodman.

Goodman didn't hesitate to form the quartet, but he didn't do it for civil rights reasons. His central interest was always the music. When the records they cut in Los Angeles became a sensation, Goodman was decided and history was made.

He viewed the color barrier as merely a pebble to kick out of his path toward the music he wanted to create. He would do what he had to do or take whatever chances he had to take in order to create the best possible music—and Hampton was integral to his quest. Hampton, Krupa, and Wilson were the guys he liked, and he couldn't accept anything less than his right to create astounding music. He already had a big band that could play arrangements with precision, now the quartet would allow him a small group that was dedicated to loose but well-controlled improvisation.

Hampton and Gladys married and moved to New York, and seemingly overnight, the Benny Goodman Quartet triumphed. With each note they played, their following grew exponentially. Their records were selling like mad and their performances had the audience dancing in the aisles. Goodman was in musical heaven.

Yet bigotry remained. Goodman did as much as he could to protect Hampton and Wilson from the prongs of racism. He would insist on contracts that allowed them to stay with the band in hotels. He would even go so far as to hire men to escort them to and from their rooms. While in New York, Goodman would hire a limo to take Hampton and Wilson to Harlem since taxi drivers wouldn't pick up black men, much less drive into Harlem at night.

Lionel and Teddy certainly faced obstacles, but with the runaway success of the Benny Goodman Quartet, those who opposed integrated bands were up against an exceptionally powerful force. Musicians, critics, and fans were driving The Four Horsemen into history.

Lionel and Teddy certainly faced obstacles, but with the runaway success of the Benny Goodman Quartet, those who opposed integrated bands were up against an exceptionally powerful force. Musicians, critics, and fans were driving The Four Horsemen into history.

There was no denying the intense effect of an integrated small group of musicians performing on the bandstand of the most popular bandleader of the era. They were the harbingers of the end of segregated jazz. In the process, Lionel Hampton became part of an ensemble that foreshadowed all that was to come when fair play began to push racist policies out of American culture. What jazz musicians had done behind the scenes for years, became public, and society was never to be the same.

AP Images

The Benny Goodman Quartet, with Benny Goodman, Teddy Wilson, Gene Krupa and Lionel Hampton, was the first band to put both black and white musicians on the same stage as part of the regular act. Nervous promoters were warned of race riots during the inaugural tour, but those fears faded as hundreds of thousands of people came out to see the band play without incident.

For the band, it was always about the music. The "Four Horsemen" of jazz would travel together for the next several years.

On the last leg of a long stretch on the road, the quartet was on an airplane returning to Los Angeles. Benny reportedly leaned over and asked Lionel what he was humming. The tune that Lionel was working on and wrote that day on the plane while traveling with Goodman was "Flying Home".

Above: The original Benny Goodman Quartet, plus a bass player, swings into a tune at Carnegie Hall in New York City, June 29, 1973. Slam Stewart, not in the original group, is second from right on bass. The quartet includes, from left, Ted Wilson on piano, Benny Goodman on clarinet, Lionel Hampton on vibraphone, and Gene Krupa on drums.

It was the last time they would play together.
Krupa passed away later that year.

International Jazz Collections, Special Collections & Archives, University of Idaho, Moscow, Idaho.

The original quartet. Eventually Krupa left to form his own band and Goodman added John Kirby on bass, Fletcher Henderson on piano and Buddy Schutz on drums.

Lionel played with Benny Goodman from 1936 - 1940. When Hampton left to start his own band, Goodman continued to show his support of Lionel by investing in The Lionel Hampton Orchestra.

LH 0210, International Jazz Collections, Special Collections & Archives, University of Idaho, Moscow, Idaho.

Lionel Hampton Orchestra

In the 1930s, Hampton recorded many classic studio sessions and was enjoying his popularity with Benny Goodman. But in 1940, he chose to strike out on his own. He and Gladys had decided to form a big band that would fulfill her vision of Hampton as bandleader. She had learned a lot about the business from Goodman and was confident that they could make a successful go of it.

They moved back to Los Angeles and formed a band comprising young, unknown, but incredibly talented musicians. While Hampton was hard at work rehearsing the band, Gladys was busy behind the scenes negotiating with instrument companies, fitting the musicians for uniforms, arranging for travel accommodations, and managing the money. They made a great team—Hampton handled the music, Gladys handled the business.

As with any new band, they had to go where the gigs were, resulting in a series of cross-country one-nighters. Even though the band was popular with audiences and had bookings all over the country, being on the road was hard—and expensive. There were some lean times during the first couple of years, but with Gladys' guidance, they were able to keep their band going. Gladys had helped Hampton to save money during the well-paid Goodman years, and so, when hard times came, the two were ready to soldier through all difficulties.

Hampton's band was put to the test while still in its infancy. At the end of 1941, they were booked at the Apollo, an engagement that would either make or break them. Hampton's incredible showmanship combined with the extraordinarily talented soloists brought the house down. They were made.

In 1942, the band had a huge hit with its release of "Flying Home" featuring Illinois Jacquet playing tenor sax, which some credit as one of the first rhythm and blues solos. The single sent the Lionel Hampton Orchestra straight to the top, where it remained for many years.

Hampton gradually expanded the show. The number of musicians increased, singers were added, and a comedy act performed at big engagements. The audience wanted variety, and Hampton always gave the audience what it wanted.

His audiences thrived on his enthusiasm and antics. Juggling sticks, jumping on drums, parading through the aisles, and playing the piano with two fingers as though they were mallets, Hampton communicated with the audience like no other had or would. His popularity continued to soar.

World renowned trumpet player and Hampton Orchestra member from the 1980s, Terence Blanchard, recalls, "Lionel's greatest musical innovation was his rhythmic approach to playing music. A lot of those guys could swing, but Lionel Hampton had a different kind of rhythmic approach to playing jazz that set him apart, no matter whether he was playing the vibes, the drums, or plucking out notes on the piano. His musical personality shined through all of that."

The audiences even extended to the White House. Always politically active, he played the inaugural galas of presidents Eisenhower, Truman, Nixon, and Reagan. And in between, he performed and campaigned for numerous other politicians. Hampton had been interested in politics since youth, but he also understood that politics affected business and that political connections would aid him in his business ventures.

©Frank Jackson/fotographz.com

Right from the beginning, The Lionel Hampton Orchestra was a training ground and launching point for some of the best jazz musicians in history. Never one to keep the spotlight to himself, Hampton gave new musicians a chance to show their chops.

Thanks to Gladys, Hampton was also getting more involved in business. He established Swing and Tempo Music and published his own compositions. He also started his own labels, Hampton Records and Glad Hamp Records. Real estate was still another venture, and one that benefited not only Hampton but countless families.

In the 1950's, times were hard for the big bands. Not only was Rock and Roll the new popular form of music, but televisions were entering more and more homes. People simply didn't go out to the clubs for entertainment as they had in the past. Interest left the big bands and moved toward small-combo

jazz. In spite of this, Hampton's music sustained. He began taking tours abroad; the Europeans were starved for jazz and could never seem to get their fill. Soon he and his band had set the worldwide standard for jazz that would last until the end of his days. He was the consummate entertainer.

Throughout his career as a bandleader, Hampton discovered and nurtured many emerging talents, some of the most prominent being Charles Mingus, Wes Montgomery, Illinois Jacquet, Dinah Washington, Dexter Gordon, Clifford Brown, Art Farmer, and Quincy Jones.

Cleave Guyton shares his experiences touring with the Lionel Hampton Orchestra:

One New Year's Eve we were hired to play at the Village Gate in New York City. At that time, Lionel had started wearing suspenders. Before the show, his attendant was helping him get dressed. For some reason, he didn't clamp his suspenders properly, and since Lionel didn't have a belt, his suspenders were the only thing to hold up his pants.

Shortly after twelve o'clock, we began playing our regular repertoire. As each tune went by, everybody was noticing that his pants were getting lower and lower and lower. (He always wore boxers.) We're in the middle of this tune and his jacket was left to keep his pants up as best they could.

He was in the middle of playing a great solo, and as he hit the high point of the solo, his pants fell all the way down to around his shoes. Nobody in the band would dare stop playing to go help him because his whole thing was, "the show must go on." He always trained us that if we were on the stage performing, that was our job. No matter what happened, you just kept playing. All the people in the audience were like, "Oh my God!" And he thought it was just because he was playing a great solo.

Another time, we were somewhere in Europe. Lionel always had this habit of going past the contracted playing time. This city had some kind of ordinance where the concerts had to stop at a certain hour because if they didn't, the promoters would get fined. At this gig, they were telling us we had to stop, but Lionel didn't care. He wouldn't stop playing until he was satisfied. These

Joe Glaser convinced Hamp to go hear a fellow Chicago native, Ruth Jones, sing. After just one set, Lionel hired her on the spot. The newly renamed "Dinah Washington" quickly became one of Lionel and Gladys Hampton's all time favorite band members.

LH 1953, International Jazz Collections, Special Collections & Archives, University of Idaho, Moscow, Idaho.

people were closing the curtain on us, and his vibraphone is at the point where the curtains come together. He was like, "How dare they!" He was holding the curtain back with one hand and playing the vibraphone with the other hand.

That was one thing that was so great about Lionel Hampton. Not only did he have a great band—the greatest musicians ever— but he also put on the best show. He had a very tight band; he could drop that band down on a dime. He could bring the dynamics down way low and bring them way up. When you got in Lionel's band, you were expected to play the hell out of those parts, and you had to do the show part too. He'd have us up there dancing, swaying side to side; we'd have to get up and walk through the audience, serenading the audience. The people loved him. The expressions on their faces, it was like they saw God or something.

Gladys's guidance and strong hand allowed Lionel and his band the security they needed to survive the lean years.

Gladys and Lionel started Glad Hamp Records with Bill Titone. He invested in a number of real estate deals, and was the decision maker in all business and legal matters.

LH 2053, International Jazz Collections, Special Collections & Archives, University of Idaho, Moscow, Idaho.

LH 2035, International Jazz Collections, Special Collections & Archives, University of Idaho, Moscow, Idaho.

Renowned for both her sense of style as well as her business savvy, Hampton's wife, Gladys, handled the negotiation and money side of the business while Lionel focused on the music.

BB King visiting Lionel while in the hospital. In 1955, the band's bus blew a tire and crashed down an embankment while traveling through New Mexico. Several members of the LHO were seriously injured and the driver was killed. Lionel was hospitalized for over two months. Visitors and telegrams poured in while he recuperated.

LH 05311, International Jazz Collections, Special Collections & Archives, University of Idaho, Moscow, Idaho.

17

Early Lionel Hampton Orchestra Band member, Oscar Peterson, at the piano. 1954, NYC, New York.

Seen here with Bob Hope (above) and Ed Sullivan (left), Lionel's music and personality brought him into contact with a number of Hollywood stars.

Universal Pictures released a short film titled *Lionel Hampton and Herb Jeffries*, which featured "Universal Stomp", "International Boogie - Woogie" and "Baby Don't Love Me No More."

18

Lionel's respect for where he came from never overcame his love of having his own band. Seen here at a 1973 reunion with Benny Goodman at the Kool (Newport) Jazz Festival in Newport, Rhode Island.

Ella Fitzgerald and Oscar Peterson (seen below in Paris) would sometimes play double bills with Lionel on their overseas tours.

The band continued to tour Europe and Asia even when jazz was falling from the public eye in America. He was greeted overseas by adoring fans and an admiring press. Seen here signing autographs on tour.

Las Vegas and Reno were popular places to play, but heavily segregated. In the early years, Lionel was not allowed to stay in many of the hotels where he was booked to play.

Seen here leaving New York for a 1971 trip to Belgium, The Lionel Hampton Orchestra had a huge European following. Lionel and his band toured over 30 countries from 1954 until his health limited his travels.

Lionel was known for his irrepressible sense of fun while on stage. This joy and exhuberance was balanced by his commitment to musical excellence.

LH 2068; International Jazz Collections, Special Collections & Archives, University of Idaho, Moscow, Idaho.

Publicity photo of Lionel Hampton and his Orchestra.

Having Fun

CONTRIBUTED BY TIM FRANCIS

Hamp loved life, and life loved him. Many others spend their existence searching for the *joie de vivre* that pulsed with every breath Lionel took. Even today, we are able to hear his vibrations of energy through his music.

Of the many lessons learned from Lionel, one that resonates, is that a 1958 Chateau Latour is just as good in a plastic cup as it is in a wine glass; the only difference is the company with whom you drink. It's no wonder why he looked forward to getting up every day. His life, like his music, was inimitable; his spirit and musical genius were completely and totally unique.

One music scholar took the time to dissect one of his compositions. In doing so, he literally wrote down each note that Lionel played, and after he finished, he concluded that it was virtually impossible for another human being to physically play the piece Lionel had just finished. In many ways it's how Hamp lived; his soul, his commitment to humanity and gentle manner allowed him to just be. We all should be so lucky.

He accepted and appreciated people from all walks of life— from his work with both Republican and Democratic presidents, to the indigenous folks he got to know on his world travels. Whether in Europe, or Asia, or here in the United States, he reached out and connected with people.

That open spirit was an infectious part of Lionel's personality, and it drew people to him. It also translated into his music and how he played the vibes and the great energy that he got from the many members of his band as well as all the others who were part of his life.

Lionel knew that he was blessed. He just wanted to entertain and to make people feel good. It was very genuine; it was part of his composition. I think he knew all along that he was part of history; that he was a living legend. At the time that Lionel went out on his own after leaving the Benny Goodman Band, there was a lot going on politically in the country with segregation and racism and so forth. Hamp was never afraid to get right in there. He was "Politically Correct" before the term was in vogue.

He and his musicians were the "rock stars" of their time. They were representing themselves and their music in such a positive and fantastic way that it became part of their constitution. That constitution then came out in his music and people responded with even higher energy. It was a cycle of giving between Hamp, his fellow musicians, and his fans that lasted for his entire life.

Lionel just loved to sit up and play music all night. He loved the company of great friends. He is also remembered for his love for champagne. In fact, one of the top champagne houses in France, Paul Goerg, honored Lionel with the creation of Cuvee Lionel Hampton. They launched the Cuvee Lionel Hampton champagne in Vienna at the Presidential Palace with the President of Austria where Lionel also received the country's highest honor. The revelry continued to New York with the domestic launch at the United Nations.

That was just part of Lionel's spirit and legacy. Lionel had a truly unique life with rare and wonderful experiences. Lionel knew what it meant to live in a state of grace—to always embrace the best of life and to put out the kind of energy that helps others, and trust that God will take care of the rest.

©Frank Jackson/fotographz.com

LH 0042, International Jazz Collections, Special Collections & Archives, University of Idaho, Moscow, Idaho.

Lionel and Jerry Lewis on stage in Los Angeles.

LH 1773, International Jazz Collections, Special Collections & Archives, University of Idaho, Moscow, Idaho.

LH 1633, International Jazz Collections, Special Collections & Archives, University of Idaho, Moscow, Idaho.

On stage, his energy and focus was all for his audience.

Offstage, his dedication and attention was for Gladys. He often said "God gave me the talent, but Gladys gave me the inspiration."

Sammy Davis Jr., Peter Lawford, Lionel Hampton and friends on stage in Las Vegas.

LH 1731, International Jazz Collections, Special Collections & Archives, University of Idaho, Moscow, Idaho.

LH 0522, International Jazz Collections, Special Collections & Archives, University of Idaho, Moscow, Idaho.

Illinois Jacquett, Buddy Rich and Lucille Armstrong visiting Lionel while he was recuperating from an operation.

Lionel Hampton, Johnny Mathis and Nat King Cole.

Mayor Ed Koch at the Kennedy Center honoring Gregory Hines, Lena Horne and Lionel Hampton.

Lionel loved to travel. His love of France was so well known, a Champagne Valley Co-op named a champagne after him!

Hampton backstage at the Apollo Theater showing his typical exuberance.

" As long as I can remember, I have known the name of Lionel Hampton. He was always a symbol for this great art form, along with the other greats: Dizzy Gillespie, Charlie Parker... to name a few... here was a man that had truly been blessed, not only with the gift of playing music, but also the ability to communicate his love for the music to so many people." - David Friesen (University of Idaho Tribute to Lionel Hampton) Below: Dizzy Gillespie and Charlie Parker.

While at Frank Sebastian's Cotton Club in Los Angeles, Hampton's showmanship blossomed. When the band started playing "Tiger Rag", Lionel would jump up on his drum like he was trying to outrun a tiger.

This move became a signature part of Lionel's shows for years.

Lionel and fan after the show.

Lionel Hampton and the Inner Circle Band rehearsing at the Piano Bar aboard an American Airlines' 747 jet.

Master Among Masters

The world of jazz is filled with giants. Louis Armstrong, Dizzy Gillespie, Coleman Hawkins, Art Tatum, Thelonious Monk, Billie Holiday—they all mastered not only their instruments but also the audience. Maybe you didn't know the notes being played or understand the complex structure of the compositions, but you knew they were the best; you knew they could make you cry or make you dance at their will.

Wynton Marsalis once said, "Jazz music celebrates life—the range of it, the absurdity of it, the ignorance of it, the greatness of it, the intelligence of it, the sexuality of it, the profundity of it, and it deals with it."

Giants hold jazz in the palm of their hand. Lionel Hampton was a giant.

Hampton was an innovative improvisationalist. He was the first person to fully transfer Louis Armstrong's innovations to the vibraphone. Because the vibraphone is an electronic instrument, notes can sustain themselves, and Hampton figured out how to make the best use of that quality. He was equally effective in using the percussive identity of the vibraphone and its ability to sustain certain notes. So when he was performing, he could play percussive phrases and then phrases in which the notes were longer. And by doing so, he could change the texture of the rhythm of his performance.

Terence Blanchard speaks to Hampton's originality: "Lionel Hampton was the modern jazz musician's dream of his time.

He picked an instrument that most people may have thought of as a glockenspiel and brought it into the realm of music, popular music, jazz to be specific, and gave it a voice where it had had no place prior to that. His musical innovation surpassed a lot of what was going on at the time he entered the music scene. His rhythmic sensibilities as a drummer carried over into his rhythmic approach to playing the vibraphone, and his harmonic expression was well beyond his years. That's one of the reasons why he had staying power. You don't have a career with that type of longevity by doing the same thing all the time."

Once he matured as a player, Hampton performed with almost all of the top-ranking players of jazz. One of the greatest compliments Hampton ever received was from Thelonious Monk. Monk was a very particular guy because he had perfect pitch; he could actually hear every single note. Monk's favorite Hampton performance was the recording session that he did with Art Tatum. Monk knew exactly what each was playing, and he liked what he heard from Hampton.

Hampton was definitely the ultimate showman, clowning around to get the audience's applause, but he was also a perfectionist. Cleave Guyton recalls, "Lionel knew every note that was supposed to be played. If there was a wrong note played, he'd get a real sour look on his face and turn around and say, "somebody in the saxophone section's playing the wrong note." He was right every time. He knew every note,

Courtesy of the Louis Armstrong House Museum

Count Basie, Lionel Hampton, Artie Shaw, Les Paul, Illinois Jacquet, Tommy Dorsey, Ed McKinney, Ziggy Elman, and Buddy Rich.

LH 0452, International Jazz Collections, Special Collections & Archives, University of Idaho, Moscow, Idaho.

every chord, how it was supposed to sound."

And he was the star, Guyton remembers with a smile. "One time, I played a really great solo and got a standing ovation. The next week we were doing a live radio broadcast, and Lionel didn't let me play one song. He was the star of the show, no one else."

Hampton recorded frequently with all-star swing artists in his earlier years. But later, he created a *Who's Who* in Jazz series on his own label. With the advancements in technology, he wanted to preserve the sounds of the greats in a format that would keep up with the times. Included in this series were featured artists such as Charlie Mingus, Gerry Mulligan, Teddy Wilson, Earl Hines, Buddy Rich, Woody Herman, Cozy Cole, and Dexter Gordon. Without question, Lionel Hampton was a jazz giant, but he never forgot that he was a master among masters.

Lionel playing with the legendary Billie Holiday.

Getty Images

CBS-TV's "The Original Rompin' Stompin' Hot and Heavy, Cool and Groovy All Star Jazz Show." Front to back, Hampton, drummer Max Roach, saxophonists Gerry Mulligan and Stan Getz, pianists Herbie Hancock and Count Basie, trumpeter Dizzy Gillespie and singers Dionne Warwick and Joe Williams.

Getty Images

"We all recognized Hamp's greatness the very first day we went to rehearsal."

— Louis Armstrong

Louis Armstrong and Lionel Hampton getting ready for a show.

Courtesy of the Louis Armstrong House Museum

Lionel's many years on the road and in studio sessions brought him into contact with a lifetime of jazz greats. When the University of Idaho put out a call for musicians to play and work with students, those greats responded in droves.

Hank Jones (left) and Herb Ellis (below) play for students at the University of Idaho festival's workshops.

"I was named after Lionel, and I wear that name proudly. My name is Lionel Frederick Cole. There are so many accolades about Lionel and all of them are true. As long as there's music, there will be a Lionel Hampton."

— Freddy Cole

Harry "Sweets" Edison and John Fadis between classes at the Lionel Hampton Jazz Festival workshops.

Dexter Gordon

© Herman Leonard Photography LLC/ctsimages.com

Dinah Washington

© Herman Leonard Photography LLC/ctsimages.com

Chuck Berry, Tony Bennet and guest greeting Lionel backstage.

AP Images

International Jazz Collections, Special Collections & Archives, University of Idaho, Moscow, Idaho.

Betty "Bee Bop" Carter got her start as a singer with Hampton's Orchestra.

International Jazz Collections, Special Collections & Archives, University of Idaho, Moscow, Idaho.

Abby Lincoln

International Jazz Collections, Special Collections & Archives, University of Idaho, Moscow, Idaho.

Al Grey

Photo by Tim Francis

Kathleen Battle, Lionel Hampton and Grover Washington together in the studio during the recording of Lionel's duet album "For The Love of Music."

"I remember well the first time I became aware of Lionel Hampton's genius. I was a freshman in high school and I heard his recording with Art Tatum. …I had never heard anything like it. Of course, Lionel Hampton is one of the great artists and musicians of all time, a great band leader, and without question, the focal figure on his instrument. …Here's to you, Hamp. Thanks for all the great music."

— Bill Charlap

International Jazz Collections, Special Collections & Archives, University of Idaho, Moscow, Idaho.

Terence Blanchard

© Herman Leonard Photography LLC/ctsimages.com

To Hamp, With Love

Read aloud at Lionel's Birthday Party at the Apollo Theater – 1996
(Transcription reprinted with permission from the University of Idaho International Jazz Archives)

Hamp, I'd like to be the first to salute you – or the next in line to salute you – for this wonderful tribute. And it takes me all the way back to 1948, when I first met you, when I was fifteen years old at the Palomar in Seattle.

I just used to sit in front of that band and watch the greatest people on the planet. You know, I wanted so much to be a part of that.

Later on, you gave me the privilege to be a part of that band with Benny Powell and Al Grey and all that distinguished company like Betty "Bee Bop" Carter and Clifford Brown and Art Farmer and Jimmy Cleveland and even Annie Ross and all those great saxophone players.

To have been in a band where I looked at the parts of the former members like "Fats" Navarro? You've got to realize what that meant to a 17 or 18 year old kid, to see Navarro's name on the parts. Joe Norman, Charlie Mingus and Wes Montgomery came through that band, which is the greatest school. [It was] the University of L.H!

From Quincy Jones

Trumpeter Clark Terry

Elvin Jones

"I remember once I went by the Paramount Theater in New York, and Hamp's Big Band was playing there. I had my horn with me and Hamp asked me to come out and play the last number, "Flying Home." They didn't tell me that at the end, an explosion would go off and smoke would fill the stage. I've always laughed about that. Lionel was always learning, always trying something new. He was always thinking about doing something different, musically. Every time on the bandstand, I would learn something just listening to Hamp. Gates, he's something else."

— James Moody

From left to right: Ruby Dee, Lionel Hampton, Tito Puente and Ossie Davis with onlookers (back).

Lionel and Thelonious
Monk backstage at the
Bandbox.

LH 0445, International Jazz Collections, Special Collections & Archives, University of Idaho, Moscow, Idaho.

Stevie Wonder at the piano with Hampton.

Photo by Tim Francis

"Thinking about the times I was on the road with Hamp and I can assure you one thing: when we got on that bandstand it was pure swing. No matter how far we traveled or how tired the band was, Hamp made you swing till you dropped. I remember we'd get off a 500 mile bus trip and Hamp would call a rehearsal. Hamp just loved to play."

— Ronnie Cuber

Ray Brown

Hampton and Dianne Reeves.

Bette Midler's revue at the Minskoff Theater in NYC, 1976, featured Lionel Hampton. Each night for the 10 week run, they brought the house down with "Flying Home."

Man of the World

Hampton was a product of America but he transcended geography with the force of achievement that comes from individual talent and will. Hampton's version of Americana was represented with sizzling force, lyrical elegance, and raucous humor. The elements of Hamp's musical Americana speak as much to people in South America, Sicily, France, or Korea as they do in the American South.

The humanity at the center of swing, when individuality is most expressive through its cooperation with and support of fellow players, was central to the life of Lionel Hampton. It was as much a part of him off the bandstand as it was in the middle of a performance.

Hampton was a visionary, both politically and socially. A Republican, Hampton campaigned for many GOP politicians, including Richard Nixon, Nelson Rockefeller, and George Bush. While his national politics may have leaned toward Republican, his local politics were focused on Democratic African American candidates. He campaigned for Democrat Lyndon Johnson and even supported former president Bill Clinton in his campaign against Senator Bob Dole. He always did what he thought was best for the country. Hampton said, "I'm first of all an American." His political activism would serve him well later in life when he needed support for his housing projects.

Hampton had always dreamed of opening a music school in Harlem, but he saw that the need for housing was greater, so he and Gladys went to work on developing a housing complex with Rockefeller's help. Sadly, Gladys passed away before witnessing the groundbreaking ceremony. Hampton threw himself into his work and oversaw the construction of the Lionel Hampton Houses and then the Gladys Hampton Houses.

Lionel's grandmother had taught him the importance of education, and he applied those lessons well. Hampton raised money for many schools and donated to several music programs. He set up the Lionel and Gladys Hampton Scholarship Fund to receive all the profits from the Lionel and Gladys Hampton Houses and set up scholarships to ensure that prospective music students got their shot at an education regardless of financial ability.

Beyond the monetary aid though, Hampton provided hands-on instruction and guidance. He was more than happy to sit down with a student and share his experiences while teaching the essentials of swing. His influence on countless numbers of student musicians earned him honorary doctorates from universities across the nation.

Even more important than education was Hampton's faith in God, and one of his greatest honors was gaining an audience with Pope Paul VI and receiving the Papal Medal for "bringing joy and happiness to the world with your music." And the church was not forgotten during his fundraising endeavors. He performed a benefit concert for the diocese of the first black cardinal in the Catholic church and raised money for Archbishop Joseph Ritter of St. Louis.

During both times of war and times of peace, Hampton often played military bases worldwide. He may not have been a soldier, but he did his duty for his country just the same. Even

L.1.1.O.A.A. International Jazz Collections & Archives. Special Collections & Archives. University of Idaho. Moscow, Idaho.

Nelson Rockefeller and Lionel Hampton
on one of their many political junkets.

movement of the African National Congress—opponents of apartheid. Hampton performed at a benefit concert in London to help raise money for their legal defense and to aid their families. The fear was that if they did not raise the money to hire good counsel, they would certainly get the death penalty. The concert was a success, and lawyers were hired. Though the men were found guilty of treason, they were sentenced to life in prison instead of the death penalty. One of those men was Nelson Mandela.

Hampton was changing the world long before it was common in America to be an activist or take a stand. His efforts to raise money for humanitarian causes, to create homes for those who needed it most, and to educate those who wanted to play a little jazz were not made in an attempt to get a headline; rather, his efforts were simply a genuine attempt to make the world a better place. And he succeeded.

when segregation forced him to play two concerts, one for the white soldiers and one for the blacks, Hampton didn't hesitate to book the gigs.

Hampton was also one of those responsible for introducing jazz, America's music, to other countries. In 1956 President Eisenhower named him American Goodwill Ambassador and Hampton took this job very seriously. His band played thirteen countries on his first official mission to increase relations between the United States and nations abroad. Included in this trip was a stop in Israel, which was the inspiration for his symphonic jazz suite entitled King David Suite. Through the years, Hampton traveled again and again to Europe, Israel, and South America, spreading jazz and making friends along the way.

These tours set him up for a truly remarkable event. In December of 1956, 156 men were imprisoned in South Africa for high treason. These men were part of the liberation

Lionel campaigned for Richard Nixon throughout his career. He was impressed by Nixon's commitment to the black community and was invited to play at four of Nixon's inaugural galas.

Getty Images

Lionel Hampton, Wally Gator, and then President Bill Clinton jamming at Lionel's 90th birthday party at the White House.

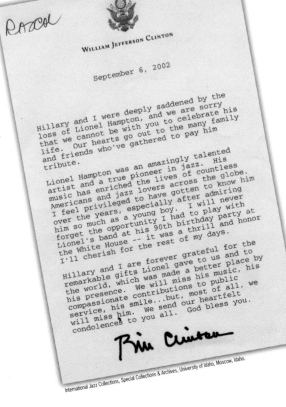

WILLIAM JEFFERSON CLINTON

September 6, 2002

Hillary and I were deeply saddened by the loss of Lionel Hampton, and we are sorry that we cannot be with you to celebrate his life. Our hearts go out to the many family and friends who've gathered to pay him tribute.

Lionel Hampton was an amazingly talented artist and a true pioneer in jazz. His music has enriched the lives of countless Americans and jazz lovers across the globe. I feel privileged to have gotten to know him over the years, especially after admiring him so much as a young boy. I will never forget the opportunity I had to play with Lionel's band at his 90th birthday party at the White House -- it was a thrill and honor I'll cherish for the rest of my days.

Hillary and I are forever grateful for the remarkable gifts Lionel gave to us and to the world, which was made a better place by his presence. We will miss his music, his compassionate contributions to public service, his smile...but, most of all, we will miss him. We send our heartfelt condolences to you all. God bless you.

Bill Clinton

International Jazz Collections, Special Collections & Archives, University of Idaho, Moscow, Idaho.

LH 0421, International Jazz Collections, Special Collections & Archives, University of Idaho, Moscow, Idaho.

From the very beginning, Lionel was a huge supporter of the armed forces. He always made time to play for the troops, even if he had to play two shows... one for the white company and one for the black.

Rudy Guiliani, Rueben Cox, Fred Brown, and Tim Francis with Lionel at a NYC party honoring Hampton.

©Frank Jackson/fotographz.com

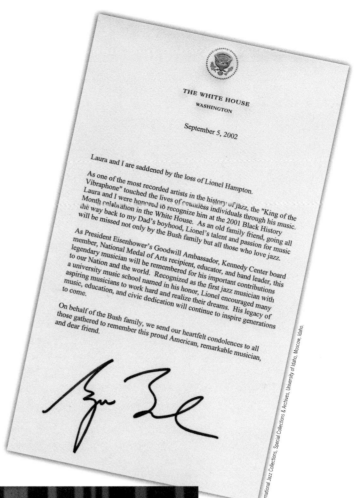

THE WHITE HOUSE
WASHINGTON

September 5, 2002

Laura and I are saddened by the loss of Lionel Hampton.

As one of the most recorded artists in the history of jazz, the "King of the Vibraphone" touched the lives of countless individuals through his music. Laura and I were honored to recognize him at the 2001 Black History Month celebration in the White House. As an old family friend, going all the way back to my Dad's boyhood, Lionel's talent and passion for music will be missed not only by the Bush family but all those who love jazz.

As President Eisenhower's Goodwill Ambassador, Kennedy Center board member, National Medal of Arts recipient, educator, and band leader, this legendary musician will be remembered for his important contributions to our Nation and the world. Recognized as the first jazz musician with a university music school named in his honor, Lionel encouraged many aspiring musicians to work hard and realize their dreams. His legacy of music, education, and civic dedication will continue to inspire generations to come.

On behalf of the Bush family, we send our heartfelt condolences to all those gathered to remember this proud American, remarkable musician, and dear friend.

International Jazz Collections, Special Collections & Archives, University of Idaho, Moscow, Idaho.

GEORGE BUSH

February 19, 2002

Dear Lionel,

I am asking Senator and Mrs. McClure, dear friends, to pass along to you my warmest greetings and congratulations as you return to Idaho for another festival honoring your fantastic contribution to American Music.

We Bushes love you, Hamp. You have been a loyal friend to three generations of Bushes, steadfastly supporting my Dad, me, and our current President.

Please know that we are with you there in spirit as you honor music and as Idaho and the nation again honors you.

Your friend who misses you an awful lot,

International Jazz Collections, Special Collections & Archives, University of Idaho, Moscow, Idaho.

LH 0974, International Jazz Collections, Special Collections & Archives, University of Idaho, Moscow, Idaho.

"Lionel was a dear friend of Barbara's and mine for over 40 years. Lionel Hampton was a national treasure. His career represents the very heart and soul of America's music, jazz. That heritage is something we as a nation need to preserve and cherish for generations to come..."
– Former President George H. Bush

45

"Hamp was never afraid to get into the mix. His perfect manner was an effective tool to building bridges in our nation's racial divide. And his sense of decency made it easy for those he encountered along the way to feel, and know, that it was ok, to just do the right thing."

— Tim Francis

Park Sheraton Hotel, NYC 1953. Hampton performs at Vice President Eisenhower's inaugural ball.

Lionel Hampton shakes hands with Japanese Princess Suganomiya at a reception in Tokyo, April 1969.

Both at home and abroad, Lionel was a favorite on the radio. Seen here performing on Voice of America in Brazil.

Hampton was always willing to donate his time and talent for a cause he believed in. He believed in helping those who could make a difference.

© Herman Leonard Photography LLC/ctsimages.com

While touring in the fall of 1957 as a Goodwill Ambassador in London, Lionel agreed to play at a benefit concert to raise money for the defense of 156 opponents of South African apartheid.

These men had been arrested and imprisoned since December of 1956. Pictured at left, the 156 accused in the South African Treason Trial.

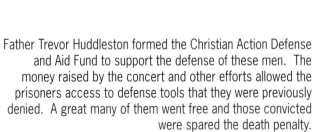

SOUVENIR PROGRAMME TWO SHILLINGS

156 accused in the
South African Treason Trial

LH B003 F053 002, International Jazz Collections, Special Collections & Archives, University of Idaho, Moscow, Idaho.

AP Images

Father Trevor Huddleston formed the Christian Action Defense and Aid Fund to support the defense of these men. The money raised by the concert and other efforts allowed the prisoners access to defense tools that they were previously denied. A great many of them went free and those convicted were spared the death penalty.

One of the men spared a death sentence was Nelson Mandela. At right, Nelson Mandela leaves the courthouse where he was being tried for treason.

Lionel and Mayor Dinkins working together. Lionel was very committed to the citizens of New York City. His Lionel Hampton Houses helped thousands of low income NYC residents find good homes.

LH 0973, International Jazz Collections, Special Collections & Archives, University of Idaho, Moscow, Idaho.

LH 1729, International Jazz Collections, Special Collections & Archives, University of Idaho, Moscow, Idaho.

Ossie Davis, Lionel Hampton, and Malcolm Wilson at the Grand Opening of Lionel Hampton Houses.

LH 2091, International Jazz Collections, Special Collections & Archives, University of Idaho, Moscow, Idaho.

Hampton playing it large with then President Ronald and First Lady Nancy Reagan at a fundraiser.

Dawaylue McCoy showing the master what he's got. Part of Hampton's legacy was his commitment to helping young people get a musical education. He donated time, talent, and money to countless scholarship funds.

International Jazz Collections, Special Collections & Archives, University of Idaho, Moscow, Idaho.

music lessons to help hone his raw natural talent. This is but one story of Hampton's dedication to the spirit of the festival and the education of young musicians.

In 1987, Hampton again emblazoned his name on musical education when the University of Idaho unveiled the Lionel Hampton School of Music - the first school of music to be named after both a jazz artist and an African American.

It was Lionel Hampton's commitment to others that created the legacy of musical education of future artists for generations to come.

Joshua Redman and Lionel

During his fifteen-plus years with the festival, Hampton performed and did everything he could to add his own brand of one-on-one education. In the mid-nineties, the university received a call from Dallas, Texas, about a young boy who idolized Hampton and wanted to play the vibes. Twelve-year-old, Dewaylon McCoy couldn't afford a vibraphone, but his school had given him a set of tone resonator bells that he turned into a vibes-like instrument. Not only did Skinner and Hampton work together to bring the boy to the festival, Hampton also invited him up on stage to play the vibes with him. While there, a retired jazz musician donated his own Lionel Hampton signature model vibes to the boy. Dewaylon also received ongoing

"The Lionel Hampton Jazz Festival will continue to be one of the foremost and significant events of its kind in the world. Built upon first-class jazz artistry, the love of and belief in jazz music and education, the support for teachers in the schools and the enjoyment and satisfaction of the student participants, the Festival continues to flourish with each passing year."

— Lionel Hampton

International Jazz Collections, Special Collections & Archives, University of Idaho, Moscow, Idaho.

Billy Eckstein

International Jazz Collections, Special Collections & Archives, University of Idaho, Moscow, Idaho.

Al Jarreau and Lionel Hampton

Doc Cheetum and Al Grey

International Jazz Collections, Special Collections & Archives, University of Idaho, Moscow, Idaho.

John Clayton.
Named Artistic
Director of the
Lionel Hampton
International Jazz
Festival in 2002.

International Jazz Collections, Special Collections & Archives, University of Idaho, Moscow, Idaho

Carmen McRae

International Jazz Collections, Special Collections & Archives, University of Idaho, Moscow, Idaho.

Jimmy Heath and
Dizzy Gillespie

International Jazz Collections, Special Collections
& Archives, University of Idaho, Moscow, Idaho.

International Jazz Collections, Special Collections & Archives, University of Idaho, Moscow, Idaho.

Lionel and Dianne Reeves

International Jazz Collections, Special Collections & Archives, University of Idaho, Moscow, Idaho.

Pete Candoli

Delfeyo and
Branford Marsalis

Dizzy Gillespie

International Jazz Collections, Special Collections & Archives, University of Idaho, Moscow, Idaho.

International Jazz Collections, Special Collections & Archives, University of Idaho, Moscow, Idaho.

Roy Hargrove, Lionel Hampton and Grover Washington

Grady Tate

International Jazz Collections, Special Collections & Archives, University of Idaho, Moscow, Idaho.

©Frank Jackson/fotographz.com

Gerry Mulligan
and Hamp

International Jazz Collections, Special Collections & Archives, University of Idaho, Moscow, Idaho.

Jon Hendricks

Herbie Mann

From left to right: Milt Hinton, Jimmy Heath, Harry "Sweets" Edison, Clark Terry - the "Golden Men."

Dee Daniels

Roberta Gambarini and Russell Malone

Ethel Ennis

International Jazz Collections, Special Collections & Archives, University of Idaho, Moscow, Idaho.

International Jazz Collections, Special Collections & Archives, University of Idaho, Moscow, Idaho.

International Jazz Collections, Special Collections & Archives, University of Idaho, Moscow, Idaho.

Lionel and his Big Band

International Jazz Collections, Special Collections & Archives, University of Idaho, Moscow, Idaho.

Left to right, John Stowell, Bucky Pizzarelli, John Pizzarelli, Corey Christensen, Russell Malone

International Jazz Collections, Special Collections & Archives, University of Idaho, Moscow, Idaho.

Shirley Horn

International Jazz Collections, Special Collections & Archives, University of Idaho, Moscow, Idaho.

Houston Person

International Jazz Collections, Special Collections & Archives, University of Idaho, Moscow, Idaho.

Freddy Cole

International Jazz Collections, Special Collections & Archives, University of Idaho, Moscow, Idaho.

Lionel Hampton
Orchestra

International Jazz Collections, Special Collections & Archives, University of Idaho, Moscow, Idaho.

Roy Hargrove and David Sanchez.

International Jazz Collections, Special Collections & Archives, University of Idaho, Moscow, Idaho.

John and Bucky Pizzarelli

International Jazz Collections, Special Collections & Archives, University of Idaho, Moscow, Idaho.

International Jazz Collections, Special Collections & Archives, University of Idaho, Moscow, Idaho.

Brian Bromburg

Diana Krall and Lionel Hampton

International Jazz Collections, Special Collections & Archives, University of Idaho, Moscow, Idaho.

StanleyTurrentine

International Jazz Collections, Special Collections & Archives, University of Idaho, Moscow, Idaho.

Nancy Wilson

International Jazz Collections, Special Collections & Archives, University of Idaho, Moscow, Idaho.

Milt HIlton

International Jazz Collections, Special Collections & Archives, University of Idaho, Moscow, Idaho.

Toots Thielmans

International Jazz Collections, Special Collections & Archives, University of Idaho, Moscow, Idaho.

International Jazz Collections, Special Collections & Archives, University of Idaho, Moscow, Idaho.

Lionel and Dizzy taking the stage

Randy Becker

Gerry Mulligan and Lionel

International Jazz Collections, Special Collections & Archives, University of Idaho, Moscow, Idaho.

International Jazz Collections, Special Collections & Archives, University of Idaho, Moscow, Idaho.

Sarah Vaughn

International Jazz Collections, Special Collections & Archives, University of Idaho, Moscow, Idaho.

International Jazz Collections, Special Collections & Archives, University of Idaho, Moscow, Idaho.

Wynton Marsalis, Ray Brown and Carmen McRae

© Herman Leonard Photography LLC/ctsimages.com

Joe Williams

Lou Rawls
©Frank Jackson/fotographz.com

One With the Ages

On August 31, 2002, the world lost a legendary jazz musician, astonishing showman, goodwill ambassador, and beloved friend to heart failure at ninety-four years old.

On September 7, a memorial service was held in honor of Hampton, this king of the vibes, this man who influenced and inspired the world. Appropriately, the event began at the Cotton Club in Harlem. After performing outside the Cotton Club with David Ostwald's Gully Low Jazz Band, trumpeter Wynton Marsalis led the second line of the procession, playing marching hymns to honor the great vibraphone master as a white horse-drawn hearse carried his remains to Riverside Church.

The New Orleans–style street procession included hundreds of people from just as many backgrounds, but all were united in their respect for the man who spent his life bringing people together through music. Though sorrow invaded the hearts of all present, this was a jazz funeral— and this memorial was a celebration, a joyous remembrance, a two-hour-long toast to honor the life and legacy of the musician and the man.

Pallbearers Bill Bergac, Norman Francis, Phil Leshin, Mike Forch, Timothy Francis, and Dr. Lynn Skinner carried his rosewood casket into the church as mourners crowded the street. The Reverend James Forbes, pastor of the Riverside Church, and the Reverend Calvin Butts, pastor of the Abyssinian Baptist Church in Harlem, presided over the service, and musicians, friends, and politicians spoke in tribute to this extraordinary man and his equally noteworthy deeds.

Former president George Bush read a letter from his son, President Bush, quoting in part, "Lionel's talent and passion for music will be missed, not only by the Bush family, but all those who loved jazz. His legacy of music, education, and civic dedication will continue to inspire generations to come."

Adding his own remarks, he then said, "For the times in which he lived, and for the timeless values he held so true, only in America could the story of Lionel Hampton be the true story of how talent and decency overcame ignorance and ill will, how opportunity and greatness ultimately yielded to perseverance, and how one life today transcends the times over which it spanned. Perhaps it speaks to the obvious, particularly here before this audience of his friends, to suggest that to know Lionel was to know joy, pure, simple joy. Like few other people I have ever met in my entire life, Lionel radiated joy, the kind of unbridled joy that permeated his music, and the kind of joy in turn which helped to shape and even define an era in jazz."

divine voices straight to the heavens. When the orchestra played Hampton's signature song, "Flying Home," the crowd could no longer contain themselves. They danced in the aisles of the church in a jubilant salute to the king of the vibes.

> *"Lionel's talent and passion for music will be missed, not only by the Bush family, but all those who loved jazz.*
> *His legacy of music, education, and civic dedication will continue to inspire generations to come."*

Wynton Marsalis, Victor Goines, Dan Levinson, and other musicians lead a musical tribute to Lionel through the streets of New York.

Daphney Reid, Hampton's caretaker in later years, read his favorite verse, Psalm 100, which begins, "Make a joyful noise unto the Lord, all ye lands. Serve the Lord with gladness: come before his presence with singing." And of course, the music dominated. The Lionel Hampton Orchestra echoed the magnitude of the man and escalated the emotions of the crowd. Saxophonist Illinois Jacquet shared stories and offered up his praises in a rendition of "Memories of You" along with Hank Jones.

Wynton Marsalis had a tear in his eye as he performed "Midnight Sun." Jon Faddis, Roy Hargrove, and Cyrus Chestnut swung powerfully for "Hamp's Boogie Woogie." And Carrie Smith, Lil Howell, and Sharlene Nelson sent their

Rev. Forbes ended the service with words of inspiration: "Lionel Hampton has played his song. He has lived his life. He now goes to celebrate in a higher sphere. Yet those of us who remain are called upon to do what Lionel always attempted to have done. When he played, he wished to awaken the song that is in the hearts of all of us. Lionel would like it to be known that there is a song yet in you that must be sung or must be played."

Hampton was buried at Woodlawn Cemetery in the Bronx, at rest and at home surrounded by Miles Davis, Duke Ellington, Coleman Hawkins, and Irving Berlin. He will be missed.

©Frank Jackson/fotographz.com

Tim Francis, Johnnie Cochran, and Norman Francis follow with hundreds of mourners behind the horse-drawn hearse from the Cotton Club to the church.

President Bush and the Rev. Dr. Forbes
sharing stories about "Hamp."

Representative Charles Rangel remarked during the memorial, "There's a
great party going on up in Heaven. They are jamming I am sure."

©Frank Jackson/fotographz.com

AP Images

The Reverend Dr. James A. Forbes, Jr. leading the mourners in the opening prayer.

Words of celebration and comfort from the Reverend Dr. Calvin O. Butts, III.

"While (Lionel's) death occasions sorrow, it should also inspire joy at the recognition that he — rising up out of our up-and-down democracy, stepping through the walls that held people back, and introducing a nearly toy instrument to the world as something upon which profound statements could be made — proved how great our nation is."
Stanley Crouch Obituary — Daily News, NYC, NY Sept 9, 2002

Over 2500 mourners flocked to the Riverside Church.

©Frank Jackson/fotographz.com

Entrance:	David Ostwald's Gully Low Jazz Band
Welcome and Prayer:	The Rev. Dr. James A Forbes, Jr.
Occasion:	The Rev. Dr. Calvin O. Butts, III
"Oh Precious Lord" (Thomas A. Dorsey)	Carrie Smith and Cyrus Chestnut
Remarks:	President George H. Bush
"Soul Serenade" (C. Ousley, L. Dixon, K. Curtis)	Lionel Hampton Orchestra
Reading of Psalm 100:	Daphney Reid
"Draw Me Oh Lord" (D. Baroni, arr. S. Minatee)	The Voices of Jubiliation Sharlene Nelson, Soloist
"Holding On" (D. Love-Coates)	The Voices of Jubiliation Lil Howell, Soloist
Remarks:	Rep. Charles Rangel
"Hamp's Boogie Woogie" (L. Hampton/M. Buckner)	Lionel Hampton Orchestra Jon Fddis, Roy Hargrove and Cyrus Chestnut
Remarks:	Bob Hoover University of Idaho President
"Lord I Want To Be A Christian"	Hank Jones
Remarks:	Congressman John Conyers, Jr.
"Midnight Sun" (L. Hampton/S. Burke/J. Mercer)	Lionel Hampton Orchestra Wynton Marsalis
Remarks:	Timothy B. Francis
"Memories of You" (E. Blake/A. Razaf)	Illinois Jacquet and Hank Jones
Remarks:	Stanley Crouch
"Flying Home" (L. Hampton/C. Christian/E. Sampson/B. Goodman)	Lionel Hampton Orchestra
Closing Remarks and Prayer:	The Rev. Dr. James A. Forbes, Jr.

Memorial Service
for
Lionel Hampton
(1908 - 2002)

9 a.m. Saturday
September 7, 2002

The Riverside Church
490 Riverside Drive
New York, NY 10027

Musicians, world leaders, writers, dancers, artists and friends gathered in Harlem on Sept 7th, 2002 to mourn the passing of Lionel Hampton.

Other services were held in Idaho, New Orleans, Detroit and around the world.

Roy Hargrove, Jon Faddis and Lance Bryant playing "Hamp's Boogie Woogie."

Cleave Guytan and the Lionel Hampton Orchestra.

Johnnie Forges and a Cotton Club Dancer.

Clark Terry

Wynton Marsalis and Cyrus Chestnut
in the vestibule of Riverside Church.

Illinois Jacquet (seated) and Hank
Jones played "Memories of You."

"It is difficult to find the words to describe the deep sadness that I have today. In our more than 50-year relationship ... Lionel Hampton was a mentor, collaborator and friend to me. Hamp was the consummate jazz artist.... I cut my teeth writing arrangements for Lionel Hampton, and there was no better school in the world than the Lionel Hampton Orchestra. He taught me how to groove and how to laugh and how to hang and how to live like a man."

— Quincy Jones

Pall bearers (starting from lower left)
Norman C. Francis, Dr. Lynn Skinner,
Phil Leshin, Bill Bergac, Mike Forch and
Timothy Francis leaving the church.

©Frank Jackson/fotographz.com

The funeral parade marched "New Orleans style" through the streets of NYC lead by David Ostwald's Gully Low Jazz Band, Wynton Marsalis, Victor Goines, Wycliffe Gordon, David Ostwald, Winard Harper, Jon-Erik Kellso, Dan Levinson, John Allred, and Ali Jackson.

©Frank Jackson/Iotographz.com

As the day unfolded, more and more people came out to honor the passing of the legendary Lionel Hampton.

©Frank Jackson/fotographz.com

Awards and Honors

©Frank Jackson/fotographz.com

Lionel Hampton

2007	The Lionel Hampton International Jazz Festival receives the National Medal of Honor
2001	Harlem Jazz and Music Festival's Legend Award
1996	National Medal of Arts presented by President, William Jefferson Clinton
1995	Honorary Commissioner of Civil Rights by George Pataki
1995	Honorary Doctorate from the New England Conservatory of Music
1993	Honorary Doctorate from the University of Maryland Eastern Shore
1992	"Contributions To The Cultural Life of the Nation" award from the John F. Kennedy Center for the Performing Arts
1988	The National Endowment for the Arts Jazz Masters Fellowship
1988	The National Association of Jazz Educators Hall of Fame Award
1987	Honorary Doctorate of Music from Liege University
1987	Honorary Doctorate of Humanities from the University of Idaho UI's School of Music renamed "Lionel Hampton School of Music."
1987	The Roy Wilkins Memorial Award from the NAACP
1986	The "One of a Kind" Award from Broadcast Music, Inc.
1984	Jazz Hall of Fame Award from the Institute of Jazz Studies
1984	Honorary Doctorate of Music from USC
1983	The International Film and Television Festival of New York City Award
1983	Honorary Doctorate of Humane Letters from the State University of New York
1982	Hollywood Walk of Fame Star
1981	Honorary Doctorate of Humanities from Glassboro State College
1979	Honorary Doctorate of Music from Howard University
1978	Bronze Medallion from New York City
1976	Honorary Doctorate of Humanities from Daniel Hale Williams University
1975	Honorary Doctorate of Music from Xavier University of Louisiana
1974	Honorary Doctorate of Fine Arts from Pepperdine University
1968	Papal Medal from Pope Paul VI
1966	George Frederick Handel Medal
1957	American Goodwill Ambassador by President Dwight D. Eisenhower
1954	Israel's Statehood Award

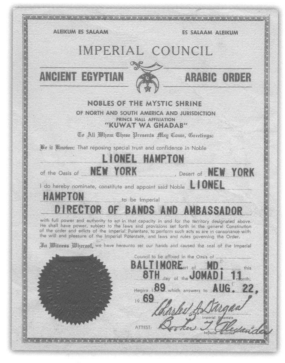

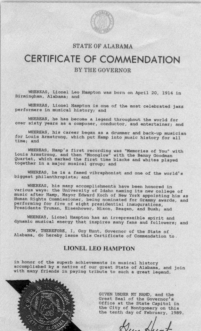

STATE OF ALABAMA

CERTIFICATE OF COMMENDATION
BY THE GOVERNOR

WHEREAS, Lionel Leo Hampton was born on April 20, 1914 in Birmingham, Alabama; and

WHEREAS, Lionel Hampton is one of the most celebrated jazz performers in musical history; and

WHEREAS, he has become a legend throughout the world for over sixty years as a composer, conductor, and entertainer; and

WHEREAS, his career began as a drummer and back-up musician for Louis Armstrong, which put Hamp into music history for all time; and

WHEREAS, Hamp's first recording was "Memories of You" with Louis Armstrong, and then "Moonglow" with the Benny Goodman Quartet, which marked the first time blacks and whites played together in a major musical group; and

WHEREAS, he is a famed vibraphonist and one of the world's biggest philanthropists; and

WHEREAS, his many accomplishments have been honored in various ways: the University of Idaho naming its new college of music after Hamp, Mayor Edward Koch of New York appointing him as Human Rights Commissioner, being nominated for Grammy awards, and performing for five of eight presidential inaugurations, Presidents Truman, Eisenhower, Nixon, Reagan, and Bush; and

WHEREAS, Lionel Hampton has an irrepressible spirit and dynamic musical energy that inspires many fans and followers; and

NOW, THEREFORE, I, Guy Hunt, Governor of the State of Alabama, do hereby issue this Certificate of Commendation to

LIONEL LEO HAMPTON

in honor of the superb achievements in musical history accomplished by a native of our great State of Alabama, and join with many friends in paying tribute to such a great legend.

GIVEN UNDER MY HAND, and the Great Seal of the Governor's Office at the State Capitol in the City of Montgomery on this the tenth day of February, 1989.

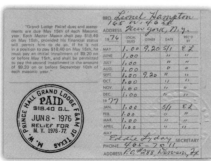

All images courtesy of the International Jazz Collections, Special Collections & Archives, University of Idaho, Moscow, Idaho.

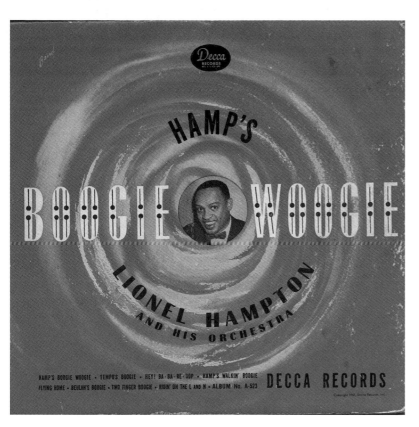

City of New York

Know ye by these presents that I

Robert F. Wagner

Mayor of the City of New York

do hereby present this

Certificate of Appreciation

to

Lionel Hampton

On the twenty-fifth anniversary of the great event at Carnegie Hall that gave jazz and the Hamp to the world. The King of the Vibes and Master of the Drums, he has always given freely of himself and his talent. A man of deep and sincere faith, he has been an ambassador to the world and a servant of the needy. A humanitarian whose acts of charity and works of skill are a credit to his profession and the American people.

In witness whereof, I have hereunto set my hand and caused the Seal of the City of New York to be affixed this sixteenth day of March, 1964.

Robert F. Wagner

Friars Club
Friar LIONEL HAMPTON

THE CITY OF NEW YORK
OFFICE OF THE MAYOR
NEW YORK, N.Y. 10007

May 10, 1971

Dear Hamp:

Mary and I have just learned the terribly sad news of Gladys' passing and offer our deepest sympathies to you and the family.

With kindest regards and prayers for your comfort during this difficult time for you all,

Sincerely,

John V. Lindsay
Mayor

Mr. Lionel Hampton
337 West 138th Street
New York, N. Y.

Most Worshipful Prince Hall Grand Lodge of Texas And Jurisdictions

Free And Accepted Masons

P. O. Box 1478 • Fort Worth, Texas

GRAND LODGE CERTIFICATE

This certifies that this lodge is a regular chartered lodge under the jurisdiction of the Most Worshipful Prince Hall Grand Lodge of Texas, F. & A. M.

I. H. CLAYBORN
Grand Master

VOLNEY B. PHILLIPS
Grand Secretary

XAVIER UNIVERSITY OF LOUISIANA

LIONEL LEO HAMPTON

In recognition of his extraordinary musical career, as a vibraharpist, drummer, pianist and orchestra leader,

In recognition of his distinguished role as a goodwill ambassador, and his abiding humanitarianism,

With pleasant memories of the happy vibes his performances have brought to lovers of music throughout the world for over four decades,

With awareness of the rich contributions he has made to music, through his influence on musical forms and the development of outstanding musicians who moved through the ranks of his orchestras and ensembles,

With appreciation for the positive image of America and Americans he created all over the world through communication in his special brand of the universal language -- music,

With cognizance of his efforts to help his people achieve a better way of life, and better living conditions,

In recognition of his stature among the foremost jazz artists of this century,

With gratefulness for his just being himself -- vibrant, a master of the skills he sought to acquire, unselfish -- a master recruiter who continues to discover and encourage young talent, indefatigable, a tireless worker for a better world ...

XAVIER UNIVERSITY OF LOUISIANA

is pleased to confer upon

LIONEL LEO HAMPTON

the degree of

DOCTOR OF MUSIC, honoris causa

All images courtesy of the International Jazz Collections, Special Collections & Archives, University of Idaho, Moscow, Idaho.

You Are Cordially Invited
to
Attend the
Awards Presentation & Fashion Show
To Announce
The National Winner of
The Third Annual
FASHION & JAZZ COMPETITION
Sponsored by Alizé
Thursday, November 17, 1988
Café 43 Restaurant
147 West 43rd Street
3:30 p.m.
Hors d'oeuvres & Alizé

R.S.V.P.
Ellen Werther
(212) 979-7800   Sponsored by Kobrand Corporation

All images courtesy of the International Jazz Collections, Special Collections & Archives, University of Idaho, Moscow, Idaho.

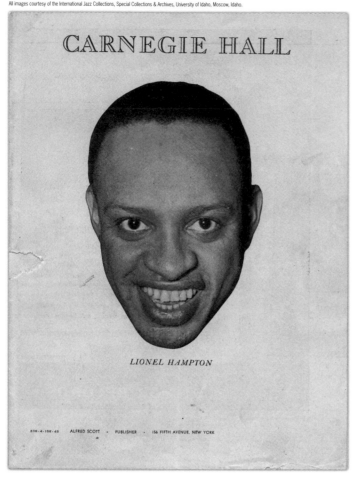

CARNEGIE HALL

LIONEL HAMPTON

336-4-15E-48   ALFRED SCOTT · PUBLISHER · 156 FIFTH AVENUE, NEW YORK

DEDICATED TO
LIONEL HAMPTON
BY THE UNIVERSITY OF IDAHO
FEBRUARY 28, 1987

University of Idaho
Lionel Hampton/Chevron

Jazz Festival 1992

Dr. Lynn J. Skinner, *Jazz Festival Executive Director*
Vicki King, Program Coordinator

Producer: Lionel Hampton, assisted by
Bill Titone and Dr. Lynn J. Skinner
8:00 p.m. Concerts
Partially Funded by the National Endowment for the Arts
February 19, 20, 21 & 22, 1992

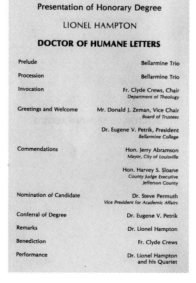

Presentation of Honorary Degree

LIONEL HAMPTON

DOCTOR OF HUMANE LETTERS

Prelude	Bellarmine Trio
Procession	Bellarmine Trio
Invocation	Fr. Clyde Crews, Chair *Department of Theology*
Greetings and Welcome	Mr. Donald J. Zeman, Vice Chair *Board of Trustees*
	Dr. Eugene V. Petrik, President *Bellarmine College*
Commendations	Hon. Jerry Abramson *Mayor, City of Louisville*
	Hon. Harvey S. Sloane *County Judge Executive* *Jefferson County*
Nomination of Candidate	Dr. Steve Permuth *Vice President for Academic Affairs*
Conferral of Degree	Dr. Eugene V. Petrik
Remarks	Dr. Lionel Hampton
Benediction	Fr. Clyde Crews
Performance	Dr. Lionel Hampton and his Quartet

FEBRUARY 23 - 26, 2005

LIONEL HAMPTON
Jazz
FESTIVAL
the legacy lives on.

University of Idaho

International Jazz Collections, Special Collections & Archives, University of Idaho, Moscow, Idaho.

"I am the luckiest man I know. I love my life. Music, travel, friends, fans and the wonderful fulfillment of helping young music students further their talents brings me great joy.

Tell me, what more could I ask?"

— Lionel Hampton

Lionel Hampton

1908 - 2002

You will be missed.

International Jazz Collections, Special Collections & Archives, University of Idaho, Moscow, Idaho.

Acknowledgements

This book would not exist if not for the vision, hard work and dedication of Tim Francis. His guidance and spirit is the soul of this book.

Thank you to the wonderful people at the University of Idaho who supplied so many of the stories and photographs in this book. Cami McClure, Interim Executive Director of the Lionel Hampton International Jazz Festival, Doc Lynn Skinner, the festival's founder, Michael Tarabulski, Archivist at the International Jazz Collections at the University of Idaho – thank you for your time and extraordinary generosity.

There are so many wonderful stories about Lionel. We would like to thank the following people for their contributions to the stories and captions in this book: Phil Leshin, Terence Blanchard, Cleve Guyton, Wally "Gator" Watson, John Clayton, Kyra Philips, Nathan Bender and Frank Jackson.

The Cadence Group is made up of many talented editors and designers who helped us craft the pages you now hold. We wish to thank: Gwyn Snider, Amy Collins, Leslie Bolton, Michelle Kelly and Melanie Zimmerman.

Out deepest appreciation to the members of the Borders Books and Music team who made this project possible. Thank you to everyone for you help and your support.

Finally, there were a number of friends of this project who put in extra hours and effort to help see this book become the best it could be. To Vanessa Prohl and Cameron Wood of The Darkroom in New Orleans, Gloria Patterson, The Sher Garner Law Firm, and all of the hardworking people at the Ogden Museum of Southern Art, we extend our deepest appreciation.

Photos by Frank Jackson are available through Heriard Cimino Gallery.
www.heriardcimino.com/